Copyright © 2019 Tekkan
Artwork Copyright © 2019

All rights reserved.
First Printing, 2019
ISBN 978-1-7343510-3-3

To contact Tekkan please email:
buddhaboy1289@gmail.com

Song of Myself

"I celebrate myself, and sing myself,
And what I assume you shall assume,
For every atom belonging to me as good belongs to you . . ."
—Walt Whitman

I would like to express my gratitude for Alan Watts,
a kind of beatnik guru of the 20th century, and to Walt Whitman,
for the inspiration they have given me. — *Tekkan*

How to Read My Poems

I am an ordinary guy living a middle class life. I may imagine what it would be like to put on a wingsuit and jump off a mountain, but my stock-in-trade is the exploration of "everyday mind." I look for transcendent meaning in the ordinary happenings of daily life. I write in the morning everyday, and try to distill experience down to essentials. It is easy to overlook the instant-by-instant process of seeing, thinking, and responding to life — but in reality that is what life is.

The mind is self-interested and driven by powerful emotions. I look around and determine what to do. I judge what's worthy, and establish a list of priorities. My likes and dislikes become signposts, and if I am not careful I find myself repeating a pattern of behavior, and get stuck, narrowly seeing, feeling, experiencing — and then where is novelty?

Spring has sprung but today is chilly. I love watching the seasons change in a succession of little details, because the seasons are so much bigger than what's going on in my mind. There is always a lot going on in nature, and my practice is to open, so that more of reality may penetrate my consciousness.

I practice opening my awareness to the world inside and outside of me. Consciousness is a miracle — but I have to learn how to use the gift of Consciousness. This is what my poetry is about.

My daughter, Jocelyn MacDonald, is a wonderful artist. Her art work graces this book.

I am Barry MacDonald. I received the *dharma* name, *Tekkan*, which means, Iron Man, a settled practitioner of great determination.

— *Tekkan*

Everyday Mind XI

Even though it's
chilly today the
buds are appearing
and I've emptied the
gas from the snow blower.

I am sure the days will be warmer and
There will be tulips lilacs and roses
Within a few weeks but I cannot know
For sure how my business will go or whom

I will meet for the first time tomorrow —
And I can't foresee the quality of
Health of my family and friends — and I
Don't often see what's coming face to face

And am more likely to be surprised and
Unprepared by events — as if events
Came from behind me — and I don't know if
My thinking in the afternoon will be

Optimistic or wearied but I know
I can't escape the tenor of my thoughts.

The future is
unpredictable —
I want to face it
without encumbrance
of mind.

I get distracted when Johnnie won't stop
Yowling for his cat food and he really
Won't stop until I feed him and Kitcat
And Henry too — and they eat before me —

And then I'm thinking about answering
Letters and taking pains to be polite
In my wording while at the same time I
Am trying to remember to get stamps

When arriving at the Post Office but
When departing my hand is reaching for
My keys in my pocket and they aren't there
And I panic because I put them down

Without noticing where I left them and
Now I'm harried and can't find my car keys.

I plan the afternoon
during lunch hour
while feeding cats
eating lunch and
listening to the radio.

From the perspectives of the wizards of
Science who are unlocking mysteries
That were inconceivable a hundred
Years ago the earth is a little blue

Dot whirling in an orbit within a
Larger orbit and expanding from where
The big bang happened some billions of years
Ago — scientists know in billions of

Years the sun will expand to burn the earth
And then to consume the earth within its
Expansion — but these facts have little to
Do with how I may choose to live my life —

The buds are asserting the renewal
Of spring and for me spring is marvelous.

Science informs me
of how exceptional
and fragile the earth is
but doesn't explain the
miracle of life.

The wizards of science are on the cusp
Of the genetic modification
Of the type of food we eat and of the
Quality of human we can birth and

In the future it's possible that we
Will winnow out diseases in the womb
And select for strength and intelligence and
Who could argue against the relief of

The suffering that comes with disease and
Wouldn't it be wonderful to upgrade
Human capability if only
We could identify the genome that

Prioritizes compassion over
Conquest and wisdom over foolishness.

Exponential change
is pitting advancing
technology
against
comprehension.

I transmit thoughts into trained impulses
And my fingers tip tap on tiny keys
And electricity transforms my thoughts
Into bits of information that are

Sequestered into files — and from my phone
I may send my thinking through the air and
Instantaneously it may arrive
On the opposite side of the earth — but

The transmission of ideas — quicker
Than the Greek God Mercury — says nothing
About the foolishness or wisdom of
My ideas — only that thoughts may be

Atomized and launched at the speed of light
As if they were photons of consciousness.

Maybe the cosmos
is full of quanta of
consciousness we
haven't yet learned
to understand.

I bought a mower a year ago and
It was idle throughout the winter but
Today it needed oil and gas and I
Became disoriented because it

Looks different from the old mower — which
I used for ten years — and when I replaced
The air filter I was pleased because a
Screw driver wasn't necessary and

The filter was easy to insert and
I tilted it over to empty the
Oil and the oil didn't empty but
I put in the oil anyway and then

I realized I put the oil where the
Gas should go and now I have a problem.

I pulled the cord
and pulled the cord
but it wouldn't start
and what do I do
now?

I like to parcel my stupidity
Into manageable increments as
It's never a good thing to deposit
An enormous clump of idiocy

Into a single event everyone
Can see — I'd like to be the only one
To recognize that I've done something dumb
So that I may with anonymity

Correct myself before anyone knows
I'm not the genius I purport to be —
And anyway the mower has two holes
And I guess I am not the only one

To pour the oil where the gas should go
And I hope never to do that again.

It's good I have
mechanically
minded friends who
know how to drain
a carburetor.

May is not May without warming days and
The temperature stayed stubbornly cold
Through all of April and we were not free
From the threat of snow so much later in

Spring and the grass is greening and the buds
Are appearing and the birds have returned
From their southern migration and I saw
A robin bobbing on a twig of my

Apple tree and I marveled that the plump
Little robin would choose such a tiny
Twig and the morning is chilly damp and
Overcast and the people I talk to

Are grumbling May is not May without
Warmer temperatures but here we are.

The weather is
an envelope
influencing
my moods.

The coniferous pines and the apple
Trees on my property have become more
Annoying year after year as they scratch
The skin of my arms and shoulders and draw

Blood and as they knock me on the head in
Passing as I mow my grass once a week —
So I've determined to take up a saw
And dismember their lower limbs and bag

The limbs to be disposed of — as I have
Been lazy and have stooped and dodged between
Their branches because I was unwilling
To do a day of extra labor to

Clear my way — but the trees are aggressive
And have taken up available space.

Grasping space and
imposing on each other
is what we do
struggling to
live.

Buds on the trees are unfolding into
Leaves again — for another season of
Breezes — the grass is greening and rising
Up — the sunlight is warming my face for

The first time — the clouds are very high and
Are flowing into feathery wisps in
The currents of the air — and there are tulips
Blooming into splashes of yellow and

Red on the east side of my house — but I
Find myself remembering how high the
Snow accumulated at the end of
The driveway — and I'm anticipating

The mosquitoes and the humidity
And the weekly chore of mowing the grass.

I am a teeter-totter
of sensations
and moods.

A boy on a walk in Iowa was
Curious about an odd-looking stone
And the stone fit snuggly in the palm of
His hand and the stone had been chipped and flaked

And it was weighty and edged and fashioned
For cutting and scraping and maybe the
Stone had laid on the ground for a thousand
Or ten thousand years — was buried under

The dirt and unearthed or was exposed to
Unnumbered starry nights obdurate to
The wind the snow the rain and the glare of
The sun until a boy in Iowa

Noticed an odd stone on the ground — and its
Weight and shape within his palm were perfect.

Stress
hunger
vigor
purpose
intelligence.

My hands are healing from the pokes and scrapes
They got when I was grabbing and sawing
Bending and breaking the lower limbs of
A pine tree that needed trimming — and an

Index finger swelled and itched yesterday
But today it's OK — and the red and
Puffy little wounds that dotted my hands
Have hard scabs today and the soreness and

The weakness in my fingers are gone — and
The larger branches are stacked on the street
And the branches with hard little needles
Are organized in bags along the street —

And this morning my fingers are tapping
On keys and words are forming into lines.

I determine
what to do and
my fingers are
essential
instruments.

My home isn't impressive and wouldn't
Generate much money on the market —
And after twenty years there are many
Repairs I need to do when there's time — though

Some of the problems involve carpentry
And electrical skills that I don't have
And there are handymen but they do need
Paying and I don't have the money so

I am learning to live with a door that
Doesn't close properly — but these are the
Rooms where my children had their birthdays where
They returned after school and I can't know

The details of their secret thoughts but here
Are the rooms that sheltered my family.

The presence
preceding
the absence
sanctifies
a home.

Am I hypnotized believing there is
A separation between my thinking
And behavior and what happens to me
In the events of my life — as if I were

A bystander blindsided by chaos
A victim of random circumstances
Not taking responsibility for
The creative power of my thinking —

Ignorant of how much the world reflects
My attitude — so much so that if the
Patterns of my thinking were different
Experience would be transformative —

Life is wild and unpredictable and
Somehow I am in the middle of it.

My dreams are wild
and unpredictable —
am I creating dreams
or are my dreams
creating me?

While my lilac bushes aren't very thick
It's hard to mow the grass underneath them
Or to rake the leaves surrounding them as
Their branches fork at odd angles and each

Branch will sprout many shoots — and because the
Bushes aren't very thick at a glance it
Seems that nothing is in the way — but when
I approach them suddenly I am stopped

Tangled and scratched and held at a distance —
And if I can reach the leaves under the
Bushes the rake is caught in a stubborn
And interlocking net of sinewy

Defiance as I encounter the wild
And resourceful life of lilac bushes.

I imposed order
and symmetry
on the periphery
with a ladder a saw
and a hedge clipper.

Most of us at the table were members
Of the divorced people's club and we were
Discussing the rites of passage with a
Frightened initiate and opinions

Were offered that it's better not to use
Lawyers because only the lawyers gain
From the escalation of expenses
But sometimes it's true a belligerent

Will resort to lawyers with the purpose
Of exhausting the resources of the
Opponent but it was humbly proposed
Demonization of the other is

Best avoided — negotiation is
Better for the sake of children involved.

A youthful marriage
is a gamble that
compatibility
will persevere
over self-interest.

A radiance is descending from an
Open sky and the grass is rising up
And the buds are unfolding and there is
A single brilliant cloud floating along

And a breeze is stirring the branches — the
Nascent leaves are wafting — and the birds are
Darting about — on the calendar there
Shouldn't be a day designated as

The day that spring arrives because that day
Is unpredictable and today is
Saturday and I'm not strategizing
About making money and I can feel

My body is responding to the sun
With irrepressible liberation

My skin is responding
to warm sunlight
to breeze on my face
and the weight of winter
is evaporating.

Learning how to make decisions that are
Productive and are not self-destructive
Resembles being disoriented
Within my own personal labyrinth

And there needs to be tension in my life
And fear is an effective stimulant
But paralyzing anxiety or
Haphazard reaction is frustrating —

I am grateful for the solitude that
Surrounds me because it's good to listen
To my chattering mind and to burn the
Chaff with the fire of my attention — and

There is a deeper part of me founded
On a quiet discerning watchfulness.

There is a
wellspring of
essential
enthusiasm
directing me.

I don't begrudge the critical voice its
Imposing place within my awareness
Because I need a check on selfishness
And a sense of justice and decency

But it's easy to belittle myself
And to disparage the things I have done
And nothing is more destructive of my
Peace than persistently negative thought

And the daily tenor of my thinking
Has the capacity to destroy my
Chances for happiness if I give my
Punishing monologue too much power

But I don't have to be alone in my
Thinking — I can always talk with my friends

Without
circumspection
gentleness
patience
love I'm
lost.

Time is segmented artificially
Into seconds minutes hours and into
Days weeks months and years — but from another
View segmenting a day is natural

For we are bound to a sense of time marked
By the rising and setting sun and by
The repetition of seasons with the
Flowering trees and the melancholy

Of the turning of the autumn leaves — and
We are captivated by the knowledge
Of death beyond which there is only a
Terrifying ignorance as each of

Us knows every human face is destined
To dissolve and disappear into dust.

I accept ignorance
and choose to believe
life resurrects
consciousness continues
and there is no ending.

Metamorphosis is a fancy word
Meaning the morphing of one form into
Another and it happens all the time
And the sun is the instigator and

The sky is its theater — and the clouds
May gather and darken quickly and a
Sudden downpour of rain may transform the
Day — and every year there are the few days

When the sun showers warm sunlight again —
No matter how long the dreary winter
May persist — and the leaves appear — and the
Flowering trees bloom again with white pink

And red blossoms — and the tulips had a
Blooming and now their petals have fallen.

I morph from
expectation
confusion
frustration
curiosity
elation.

A friend was on a dig in Israel
With his friend Ofer at an ancient fort
And Ofer unearthed a hammered golden
Ring that came from the height of the Roman

Empire two thousand years ago and
Ofer wore the ring on his pinky for
Eight years until Ofer was asked about
The ring at a conference and to my

Friend's amazement Ofer gave the ring to
The person who asked about it because
Ofer said the ring was taking too much
Of his consciousness — as an example

Ofer enjoyed an unexpected gift
And he learned how to pass the gift along.

The gift is an
unexpected
liberation.

The apple blossoms were in the puddles
On the pavement after the pelting of
The rain — looking like the confetti on
The street after a parade — but we missed

The parade this year as the blooms were just
Starting to appear when an overnight
Downpour broke the connections of petals
With the trees and I feel a little sad

That the joyous parade of my driving
By the flowering trees has passed me by
This year because I love seeing the blooms
As a celebration of beauty that

Always accompanies the return of
Spring and the resurrection of the trees.

But now I see
many of the trees
have yet to reach
their full flowering and
I'm just being gloomy.

It's been chilly far later into spring
Than at any time I can remember
And for the last few days it's been raining
But the leaves are almost fully grown and

They appear gradually but when they
Are grown they are always freshly pristine —
And on any day there are details that
Need attending to with people and work

And it would be easy to overlook
The return of the leaves for another year
Of productive sunlight — but what I love
Is the peaceful sound of the breeze stirring

In the branches and sighing through the leaves
Which suggests there's no need to be anxious.

The breeze in the leaves
is background music
whispering and
peaceful.

A student doesn't have to travel far
To find the lessons that are genuine
And the suggestion I read this morning
Was that there are only two emotions —

Fear and love — and that irritation and
Jealousy and anger — or gratitude
And forgiveness and curiosity —
Derive from the one root or the other

And it's easy to live ignorantly
To be arrogant and to believe I
Am doing as I should be doing and that
Anyone in my place would do the same —

And there is no end to indulged anger
But there is resonance in gratitude.

The resonance of
gratitude
forgiveness
curiosity leads
to a better life.

It's easy to think my thoughts are private
And that I can't be blamed for angry thoughts
But anger isn't easily contained
And my thinking ripples into the world

And the world ripples in response to me —
And so I watch the quality of my
Thinking and I know when my balance is
Off — and it is possible to become

Quiet through the practice of watching thoughts
And I can fortify my consciousness
With persistence and patience — because I
Know that I will feel differently in

A little while as circumstances change —
And I see the world never stops changing.

There is so much
going on all around me
in a single moment
I can't possibly
comprehend.

The wind in the leaves is too rough to be
Poetical and the sky is filled with
Such gloomy and low-hanging clouds moving
Quickly and raining spontaneously

And the air has been stubbornly chilly
Too long into spring for my preference
But the leaves are fully grown and the birds
Are darting about in a violent

Wind — like so many other things in life I
Don't get to choose what the weather will
Be and I have to make do with what comes with
A daily view of metamorphosis —

Is it silly to wonder whether the
World would exist without my being here?

I guess the question
depends on whether
my consciousness is a
drop of a bigger
consciousness.

I am a drop of consciousness and what
I don't know extends beyond what I do
And I may easily be discouraged
When I am feeling lonely and afraid

And when I am isolated sometimes
I create explanations in my head
About why a person said hurtful words
That impacted and summoned my anger

Or when I can't find a way into a
Conversation among my friends I may
Believe myself unworthy of friendship
And I am lost in silent arguments

So it is my practice to forget that
I am only a drop of consciousness.

A drop of
consciousness
needs to find
a way to flow
in the river.

I won't say that Johnnie is becoming
Seven pounds of nuisance because saying
So isn't nice — but just between the two
Of us — he is — as I was enjoying

A dream this morning immersed in a world
Of swords and spears and warriors when I
Heard the intrusion of a yowling cat
Demanding food outside of my door and

He's becoming more insistent over
Time and he's starting earlier in the
Morning and I can exclaim JOHNNIE NO
But Johnnie won't stop until he's been fed

So I get up and carry him to the
Bathroom deposit him and shut the door.

Johnnie
should think
about his
behavior and
whether it's
propitious.

To me the blooming of cherry blossoms and
Lilacs are worthy of celebration
And I don't do anything overt to
Mark their appearance except to notice

How they lighten my spirit — and the breeze
Will envelope their sweet scents and waft it
Away — and very soon the breeze will take
The delicate petals and flowers and

Scatter them on the ground — and I wonder
How do the flowers blossom when through the
Winter the branches are bare and the trees are
Frozen — and I marvel at the absence

Or the emptiness from which everything
Appears and to which everything returns.

When blossoms
appear the bees
get busy — but do
they also rejoice?

There is a shifting in spring into a
Sunny brilliance when the light sparkles on
The river as the dreary weather has
Dissipated — and the sun becomes a

Magical source of resurrection — and
The dandelions and the creeping Charlie
Appear in my yard — and the trees by my
Driveway present their apple blossoms — and

I'm not sure whether the newly grown leaves
Are brightest in the spring or whether their
Dramatic reappearance lends them a
Magnificence that wears off over time

But the sighing of the breeze in the leaves
Is whispering such soothing assurance.

The curving of space
by the gravity of the
sun tips the earth
around the sun
predictably.

A storyteller assumes the powers
Of a deity weaving with threads of
Meaning into the stories of a Queen
Of a dragon and of a bastard who

Is really of royal birth — but once the
Tale's been told the mystery is
Gone and the fate of the actors is known
And the retelling can only rehearse

A familiar conclusion — but we need
Storytellers and if we are smart we
Will choose the tellers who inspire and
Ennoble because our authentic lives

May be dispiriting and it's good to
Weave with the threads of hopeful energy.

Dissipating or
accumulating
enthusiasm is
determinate.

Writers used to be confronted by the
Emptiness of a sheet of paper but
Today the paper has been replaced with
A blank computer screen with a blinking

Cursor — but the challenge is exactly
The same — what thoughts do I have this morning
That are worthy of communication —
Invisible raindrops are falling from

A gray sky and my circumstances are
A little gloomy but I'm not bound by
Moodiness because writing poems is
An enthusiasm generating

Machine for me as I've discovered a
Method for grasping satisfaction.

There are roots of
curiosity and
gratitude about
simply living that
flower.

I'm in my element most of the time
And swimming along without a worry
As I wake up early every morning
And after doing some chores I will sit on

A cushion and meditate for a while
Which gives me an indefinable sort
Of energy that mitigates the wear
That comes with the ordinary ups and

Downs — and I love the freedom that arrives
With the sunlight of morning clarity
When my mind percolates with probing thoughts
And I may indulge curiosity

Until I see another damn letter
From the Internal Revenue Service.

Suddenly I'm
a goldfish in
a little bowl with
an idiotic cat
after me.

When I close my eyes when facing the sun
I see a marvelous red light that is
The sunlight filtered by my eyelids — and
My face is bathed in the beating of the

Sun and after a few minutes I am
A little dizzy — and the red sunlight
Warming my face helps me to imagine
Myself a tomato under the sky

With nothing to do all day but listen
To the drone of cars and machinery
In the distance and absorb the force of
The persisting sunlight enveloping

And tranquilizing me in unceasing
Dissolving forgetful meditation.

Raindrops
inescapably
pattering
my face
would be
difficult.

Politics is an insider's game and
The players rely on the fact that most
Citizens don't have the inclination
Or the knowledge to follow the details

Of issues and it's advantageous to
Accuse opponents of dishonesty
And to smear their reputations with the
Most outrageous slanders — and the players

Know that they are lying — and perhaps they
Smirk at notions of Hell — but once they start
There can be no relenting from lying
Accusing and empty posturing because

The momentum is unforgiving and
They are terrified of exposure.

They are riding the
tiger of politics
desperately
afraid and
grasping.

Not every thought I have is worthy of
My attention and some thoughts are burning
Cinders that light upon my skin and hurt
And I have to practice flicking those thoughts

Away instantly or otherwise I
Will find myself swirling inside of a
Malignant obsession with vacant eyes —
And I can't at the moment prevent a

Perception from rising within my mind
But with the focus of my attention
I can practice letting go of anger —
And what I choose to say or do is a

Confirmation of my intentions and
Being careful is the art of living.

The harmony of
living is a happy
mixture of what
happens and how
I think about it.

The art of living is the releasing
Of dispiriting thoughts and the seeking
Of inspiration and when I saw the drops
Of water hanging from the crooks of my

My apple tree after a rainy day
In February I was astonished
By the sight of the hundreds of drops of
Water refracting the sunlight in a

Tree in a season when usually
Everything is frozen and burdened by
The snow — I realized that the world is
Fluid and unpredictable — even

In midst of difficulty there is
The surprising poignancy of beauty.

Anticipating
inspiration is
like snatching
a bird
in flight.

The freedom of mind to see a blue jay
A red wing blackbird or a cardinal
And to see them without a thought getting
In the way is wonderful — I touch them

With my sight on the fly and I am left
To wonder at the beauty on the move
About me — I like to leave my thinking
Behind me for a while because it's so

Easy to be obsessive and then
I am not using my eyes properly —
And when I am not the center of my
Attention the unfiltered impact of

The world makes its influence felt in waves
Of difficulty sorrow and beauty.

My friend Judy
directed me
to a silky
little bird — the
cedar waxwing.

The blooming of the lilacs has nothing
To do with me as I am not lifting
A finger to make it happen as the
Purple flowering appears briefly once

A year and the sweet scent doesn't travel
Far and when I am properly focused
On the details of my business and the
Common unpredictability of

Cooperating with people lilacs
Are of no assistance to me except
That I look forward to their blossoming
And their scent in the middle of winter

And their coming and going brings such joy
And joy in passing is worth indulging.

Lilacs of
various shades
are predicable
in a fluid and
disappointing world.

While walking from the height of the north hill
Down through Stillwater and south along the
River I ascended up and across the
Magnificent Crossing Bridge spanning the

River — and a thought came to mind that I
Could read one day's collection of essays
From America's major newspapers
With the intention that I would quote the

Snarky and accusatory writing —
I would write an essay exposing
The corrupting and dispiriting weight
Of commentary that Americans

Are reading on any random day — but
I realized that's the nature of news.

Americans artfully
spanned a river valley
at a great height and
Americans have an
appetite for venom.

A dragonfly has extraordinary
Eyes that wrap around its head and allow
It to see behind and below on the
Fly and each eye deploys thirty thousand

Lenses and each lens captures an image
Of the fluid world and they combine to
Give it extraordinary sight — and the
Dragonfly can follow the flight of a

Fly and with four angled wings capable
Of hovering and flying backwards it
Can snatch the fly from the air and slice it
With its mandibles and eat the fly while

Hovering — and it sees the colors of
Ultraviolet light that I can't see.

But I can't
imagine getting
many dates if
I had a dragonfly's
head.

I had the curiosity and time
And a search on Google informed me that
The ruby-throated hummingbird flies straight
And fast — but can stop instantly — hover —

And adjust up and down — hummingbird hearts
Are beating twelve hundred times a minute —
And they are breathing two hundred fifty
Times a minute — and they are licking their

Nectar ten to fifteen times a second —
And I can hardly believe the essay
Saying that a dominant hummingbird
Has the gumption to chase the jays and crows

And the hawks away from a feeder once
The hummingbird has taken possession.

I could put up
a hummingbird
feeder and
hummingbirds
would come.

The bee hummingbird is an exquisite
Native of Cuba with fluttering wings
Iridescent feathers and a pointy
Little beak and the bird and its nectar

Are coincident because one could not
Exist without the other — just as I
Could not exist without the sky the rain
And the earth — this is what the earth has come

To with hummingbirds and flowers and rain
And people — as we are emerging out
Of the trillions and trillions of degrees
That was coincident with the little

Space that was expanding rapidly that
The scientists are naming the big bang.

The bee hummingbird
and I are a
continuation a
permutation of
the big bang.

See what the cosmos is capable of
On the earth as I am an awakened
Drop of consciousness under a sun — and
As a drop of consciousness absorbed in

Kaleidoscopic rivers and oceans
And drops of rain I am at home in the
Liquidity of the earth as the earth
Is incarnating and dissolving forms —

And I can appreciate the flouncing
And the prancing of an opalescent
Peacock and the slithering sinuous
Motion of a garter snake — and in the

Brilliance of an open summer sky I
Spot the floating of a cottonwood puff.

I wonder whether
consciousness comes
within waves of
appearing vanishing
quanta.

It was time to feed the cats before dawn
And Kitcat wasn't in the house and the
Only explanation was he got out
When the door opened without being seen

And he disappeared once before last year
On a day that became rainy and I
Worried about him because he was never
Outside by himself and I wasn't sure

He'd be OK — now for the second time
He escaped and stayed away for the whole
Day — and like before in the early hours
Before dawn he yowled at a window and

I opened the door and in he came and
He flopped on the carpet triumphantly.

Maybe he pressed
open the latch
of the screed door
by standing on
hind legs.

The beating of my heart and the burning
Of the sun are cooperating — a
Supernova seeded the cosmos
With the elements of life eons ago —

And gravity formed the planets and tipped
The planets into orbit around our
Sun — and gravity crushed the mass of
The sun igniting nuclear fusion —

And a sun burning and a heart beating
Are spontaneous and simpatico
Are a mixture of the vast and minute
Collapsing into curiosity —

My body is an outgrowth of cosmic
Proportions — but where do questions come from?

Am I beating
my heart or is
the cosmos
beating it?

There are assumptions within my thinking
That are unnoticed within rhythms and
Rhythms of thinking — and sometimes I am
Able to recognize that my thinking

Is convincing me that everything is
Chaotic and that I need to impose
Myself and make things happen and thereby
Gain satisfaction — and sometimes I can

Recognize that what is emanating
In the form of my rhythmic thinking is
Resonating into what's happening
Around me — and that sometimes there is a

Painful dissonance and sometimes there is
Harmony — while everything is flowing.

Thoughts are like raindrops
blowing on a lake —
with few harmonies
with many chaos.

Are the burning sun and a beating heart
Separate phenomena or are
They continuous with each other
Proceeding from the original source

That is called the big bang — though however
It happened there couldn't have been a sound
Because for a sound to register there
Needs to be an atmosphere to transmit

Vibrations and there needs to be ears and
Minds to transform the vibrations into
What could become a bang — and however
It happened there was nothing beforehand

But afterwards something was expanding
Radiating vibrating emerging?

Sun burning
heart beating
ears hearing
mind thinking —
are they all vibrations?

My head is a gourd of the cosmos — and
Thoughts are emerging from behind my eyes —
Or at least that's how it appears to me —
And scientists have discovered that the

Vibrations in my brain are transforming
Photons arriving from the sun into
My perceptions of colored light — and if
My brain were not transforming vibrations

There wouldn't be any light at all but
Only transitory vibrations through
Emptiness — and it's hard imagine
There being neither brightness nor darkness

And it's hard imagine the absence
Of colors — but that's what emptiness is.

My cosmic gourd is
creating
sight
sound
smell
touch
taste
questions.

While driving around and observing the
Familiar scenery on the highway
And in Stillwater I am listening
To Alan Watts on a disk saying that

I am casting a net over the world
Dividing and classifying the world
Measuring and quantifying the world
While everything is continuous — and

In the natural world there is no such
Thing as an inch — or a mile — or a line
Of longitude — and time doesn't come in
Seconds or minutes but — truly — the trees

And the horizon wiggle — the birds wiggle
And people are especially wiggly.

Can I pick up
an inch by the
edge from the
ground and
pocket it?

The trees were quiet a moment ago
But now they are sighing in a breeze —
Streaming gray clouds were converging and
Concealing and the sun — then they were

Dispersing and revealing the sun — and the
Light was momentarily brilliant — but now
The gloom and the chill are returning as
The clouds are obscuring the sun again —

My hands were on a steering wheel as I
Was turning corners on the streets driving
To arrive at my desk — I was typing and
Deleting words uncertain about my

Direction — but now I've discovered a
Pattern while hunched in a chair composing.

Quiet and sighing
shadow and light
restless confusion
settling thought
satisfaction.

I'm not enlightened but would like to be
And I know — because I'm listening to
Alan Watts — that craving enlightenment
Becomes a guaranteed impediment —

And Alan is insisting there's nothing
I can do and no where I can go to
Penetrate the mystery — and Alan
Is saying that it may take thirty years

Or three seconds — while the evidence is
Everywhere before me — and having a
Good laugh afterwards is a natural
Result — and Alan is suggesting that

Secretly I don't want to wake up but
When I really really do — then I will.

Alan has a way
of simplifying
and clarifying
and I can't stop
listening.

A teacher in Japan talked about the
Unborn mind that is given by parents
To their children that is always present
And the unborn mind can be distinguished

Said the teacher when the students are in
The dharma hall and are listening to
A teacher and a sparrow twitters and a
A crow caws and the birds are heard as a

Crow and sparrow without difficulty
And no effort was made to hear them and yet
They were heard and this is the eternal
Mind that doesn't struggle to exist and

In America after four hundred
Years I am puzzling over his words.

Zen Master Bankei
pointed out
unhindered
bare awareness.

What does the air do to a butterfly
As it emerges from a chrysalis
Not having been a butterfly before
And discovering that it has wings — and

Does it fall and flutter as it falls or
Does it arouse itself and beat the air
With its wings to rise into the air for
Its initial flight — and is it a strain

On a butterfly's heart to push down on
The air as its beating heart is in sync
With its sashaying manner — and is the
Air the same air the gliding eagle or

The acrobatic swallow knows or is
It living in a different cosmos?

What does the
butterfly think as
it encounters drops
of rain and a
boisterous wind?

I've lived most of my life without knowing
When during the day I am most awake —
And maybe meditation is helping —
And maybe playing with words is helping —

Because I have to be flexible to
Play with words — but now I am using the
Tides of my mind — seeing clarity come —
Feeling energy — anticipating

The insights — like snatching a bird in flight —
But then I endure the ebbing of my
Energy and the ensuing dullness —
There is pleasure in surfing the tide and

In cultivating inspiration but
Then I have to let energy go.

When I am
naked in the shower
warm cascading water
summons enthusiasm
and clarity.

"Good friend for Jesus sake forbeare,
To dig the dust enclosed here.
Blessed be the man that spares these stones,
And cursed be he that moves my bones."
—William Shakespeare

When I was a student in England I
Went on a solitary pilgrimage
To the Church of the Holy Trinity
In Stratford-upon-Avon to visit

The earthly remains of the poet whose
Plays and sonnets had so inspired me
And I didn't really know exactly
What about his writing had taken root

But the inscription on his grave was a
Clue sparking recognition today — I
Adore his piercing concision and his
Passion and the play of images and

Personality — that all he gave me
Were the words — and his imagination.

When I imagine
Kings and Queens —
and clowns — it's
Shakespeare I
rely on.

I have lived with the peonies on my
Property for twenty years as they are
Rooted with the daylilies within a
Circle of largish rocks I labored hard

To establish — and my ex-wife planted the
Peonies — and I didn't know the name
Of their kind of flowering though I did
Admire their pink lush beauty — but there

Were many years when I overlooked their
Blooming and this spring I was surprised at
Their presence and noticed the oddity
Of peonies — that their overlarge blooms

Bend their blossoming to the earth giving
Them the appearance of bashful women.

Embarrassed
beauty is an
alluring ploy
mesmerizing
lustful bees.

The names we give to things are a gloss of
Our humanity so that when we see
The planets and the moons of our solar
System we say — in the manner of the

Ancient Greeks and their deities — there is
Saturn and there — Saturn's largest moon — is
Titan — and we could not do otherwise
Because the things we see must be given

Their names and thereby comprehended — and
Our sight has extended into space and
We can see that the lakes of Titan are
Liquid methane and we can understand

That the cosmos is inhospitable
To life — outside of the earth's atmosphere.

The big bang
was silent because
without an atmosphere
and without ears
there is no sound.

There is the precarious time of night
After midnight and much before the dawn
When — if I find myself awake — there is
Great difficulty in falling back to

Sleep — because once I start thinking about
My difficulties the debates I have
With me do tend to become obsessive —
But last night I heard the minutest whine

Of a mosquito coming nearby and
Going away — and once I heard it by
My ear and I slapped — and smacked my ear —
And it whined about my ear again and

I slapped and smacked my ear again — and then
I laid awake vigilant and vengeful.

Don't tell me to —
take it easy — because
that's a fatuous
phrase designed
for idiots.

I take a considerable amount
Of bother to arrive at my office
With an air of serenity about
Me by meditating beforehand and

I arrange my schedule to allow
A sacred hour of quiet so that
I can apply myself to poetry
And I settle within a comfy chair

And gaze longingly out of my widow —
And with fingers poised over my keyboard
And with my thoughts beginning to pop the
Damn phone tears my attention away and

All I hear is a recorded message
Saying — stop and listen and don't hang up.

Robocalls
everyday
like mosquitoes
are snatching
my composure.

I'm thinking I am at the center of
The cosmos and maybe everyone is
Also thinking they are at the center
Of the cosmos — which prompts the question where

Can we find the circumference — and maybe
There isn't a circumference — and I am
Questioning whether the fire knows it is
Burning itself and does the water know

It's quenching itself — and do I really
Know how I am beating my heart and how
I am inhaling and exhaling air
With my lungs — or is there a broader part

Of everyone that does these things without
Having to know the things we are doing?

And maybe
consciousness doesn't
need to remember
much beyond the
present moment?

There is a flux of consciousness in a
Day with the impetus of clarity
In the morning and the dissipation
Of energy and optimism in

The afternoon and there are the rhythms
Of a beating heart and circulating
Blood and breathing lungs continuing with
No conscious direction and there is the

Drowsy transition into sleep and the
Eerie unpredictability of
Dreams — and where would I go if I went to
Sleep and didn't wake up and what would it

Be like to awake after not having
Gone to sleep — which is what everyone does?

Fluxing
rhythmic
automatic
cosmos working
me.

The rose bush was bordering the concrete
Patio in front of the door to my
House when we came twenty years ago and
It has needed the trimming I didn't

Do until the previous year — because I
Am easily distracted and sometimes
I am lazy — but I did expend a
Little energy pruning the dead wood

Away — and now I see the rooting of
The bush has moved from its early spot to
Sprout between the cracks of the concrete and
It is a gnarly and persistent plant

Worthy of its thorns and maybe I would
Not have noticed but for its blossoming.

The rhythm at
my home is
apple
lilac
peony
pink roses.

Light and sound envelope me in waves and
The thing to know about the waves is that
There is the crest and the trough and if
I think about things from a view of an

Ocean of particles I'm swimming in
Sometimes I am an aggregation of
Particles and sometimes I dissolve into
A waving ocean vanishing and then

Appearing again — and I tend to think
Of moments as the building blocks of time
Marching to a conclusion but then I
Can see the cycles of the orbits and

The seasons as more compatible with
A crazy wavy unceasing cosmos.

Van Gogh observed
wavy reality
before quanta
became a knowable
thing.

My ability to think and move is
Not the same as a leaf emerging from
A bud and unfolding — is not like a
Peony bloom appearing in June — and

I tend to believe that trees and plants and
The sky and the river are part of the
World — and that I am something apart that
Was summoned into the world to play a

Part like an actor on a stage — and my
Soul comes from and returns to another
Realm — but maybe the world is growing me
And I am emerging out of it — like

A thoughtful peony blossom and a
Conscious cosmos is seeing with my eyes.

Maybe the cosmos
grows consciousness
like it grows
gravity and galaxies.

I like to write about the cosmos and
Peonies but it happens when I am
Waiting for the words to fit perfectly
Into a pattern of sound and grammar

And syllables — that come together like
The pieces of a puzzle — suddenly
My attention is ripped away by the
Ringing of the infernal phone — and from

Experience I know I'll likely hear
The tinny voice of a robot with a
Message of no interest to me — and I
Am primed to growl — hello — and if there's

A silence or a click when listening
To the receiver I will just hang up.

This is a cosmos
mixing peonies
and robocalls —
mosquitoes and
roses.

I sit facing my window with the sun
Rising with a wide brim straw hat grateful
That I am here with a clear mind shielding
My eyes from the bountiful summer light

And relishing the tipping point between
Coolness and the warmth of the asserting
Sun and I don't have to know very much
About what anyone else is doing

At the moment and don't have to wonder
What I'll be doing in a couple of
Weeks as I'm beginning to believe my
Beating heart and seeing eyes and warming

Skin and the birds the dragonflies and the
Sun are a perfect sphere of consciousness.

Sun penetrating
heart inaudible
ears absorbing
the printer humming
the aquarium bubbling.

If I look at the world with fresh eyes could
I forget about the differences
Between the outside and the inside of
Me — could I dispense with my habit of

Fixing on the proximity between
Me and others and could I stop taking
Possession of what's mine as opposed to
What's yours — because I have a lifetime of

Practice of making distinctions and of
Constructing an identity with the
Urgency of ignorance and fear — and
I suspect everyone else is playing

By the same rules with a ferocity
That makes playing the game so dangerous?

Just for a moment
could I dissolve
proximity and names and
even words and with a
finger touch the moon?

There is a humongous hill of ants near
The cottonwood where I was watering
The grass and I didn't think much about
Them except to see that their colony

Is extending around the cottonwood —
And then I was attending a meeting
Of my friends and waiting for my turn to
Speak while wearing a silk Guayabera

Shirt when there was a tickling under
My shirt and across my belly and I
Felt the tiny feet and knew that an ant
Was ascending to my collar bone as

I was attempting to listen to my
Friends — and not to wiggle scratch and grimace.

I am not usually
aware of the
fine hair on my
belly — but the
ant reminded me.

With the abundance of the summer sun
I can mow the grass following supper
When the leaves are sparkling with the sun
And there is not a time when I am free

From doing the chores that come with living
And the imperative of getting things
Done is something I do without thinking —
And the prominence of the summer sun

Is a pattern of a lifetime that is
Akin to a heart beating and the lungs
Breathing — as it is a pattern within
Patterns I am not manipulating —

But I'm taking the time to absorb the
Warm embrace of the reliable glow.

I imagine
myself a
marshmallow
browning outside in
and inside out.

I've been trying to keep up with my chores
And mowing the grass and feeding the cats
And watering where the grass seed was laid —
And by rushing from chore to chore I did

Prodigious work in a couple of days —
Just so I could have a carefree Sunday —
But there was rain and wind in the morning
And my cottonwood did what cottonwoods

Do — break apart and drop branches — and now
I have a tangle of weighty thick limbs
To dispose of — and how will I do this

Unexpected task without giving up
Something else I would rather be doing?

I suspect the
cottonwood is
my guru today
playing a game by
dropping hints.

My eyes are seeing perfectly well what
Is in front of them — there is rain and wind
And the trees are tossing about — but I
Can't see what's behind my eyes and can't see

The back of my head — and it would be a
Hoot to be a perfect sphere of vision
So that I could see the top of my feet
The ceiling the carpet and the doorway

Behind me — but even then there would be
An empty spot inside my spherical
Eye — and usually I don't notice
What I would call my hole of consciousness —

There isn't light or darkness inside my
Head where my thinking is percolating.

The emptiness
where my thoughts
come from is the
emptiness where the
cosmos comes from.

The emptiness behind my eyes is not
Something that I can think about because
I cannot see or grab hold of it — and
It is not even a thing — it is a

No thing — I can see the tip of my nose
And I can turn in any direction
And enjoy a field of vision that is
Limited — and with technology I

Can view galaxies and with books I can
Play with ideas that are based on things
That are within the galaxies — and I
Generate my emotions dependent

On my relations with people or things —
But I know nothing about emptiness.

Except
everything
comes from
emptiness.

There was a day forty years ago when
I was a grunt on an asphalt driveway
Crew preparing the ground for the layer
Of underlying rock that we would lay

And the natural mixture of rocky
Soil needed to be broken up so that
A foundation could be made — and they gave
Me a pickax with permission to wreak

Havoc — in an ecstasy of labor
I discovered how to swing the ax with
The continuous movement of my feet
And with the furious melody of

Unceasing circling destroying blows
Which was a workingman's enlightenment.

I became the
embodiment of
righteous
disintegrating
force.

There was a reason for the pickax that
Day as the tractor couldn't get at the
Spot and the work had to be accomplished
By shoveling and the ground was as hard

As cement and the flat end of the ax
That angles outwards is designed to drive
Into the earth and explode the earth with
The removing swing of the ax — and the

Ground was broken to bits — and shovels could
Be thrust in to remove the rocky dirt —
And on that day my body was youthful
And a joyous fierceness awoke in me

That I didn't know I was capable
Of — and decades later I remember.

I swung the ax and
Willie the crew chief
on the tractor
called me
John Henry.

Would it go to my head if I stood at
The top of a mountain wearing a wing
Suit surging with adrenaline seeing
The immensity of distance before

Me and taking a of leap of terror and
Joy to fall gracefully among rocky
Precipices as if I became an
Eagle plunging in and out of alpine

Shadows prepared for a sudden death in
Exchange for a rushing simulation
Of divinity — would I glory in
The experience and be compelled to

Do it again — to be soaring again
Exploding the bounds of humanity.

Flying in a
wing suit
would be a
high I'd never
escape.

I was minding my business eating lunch
And listening to the radio when
A grape escaped my grasp and rolled away
And I straightened my back and gasped because

This sort of thing has happened before with
Peanuts and grapes — and I know as far as
Potential trauma goes a lost grape is
Small potatoes — and a missing grape is

More of an inconvenience as I
Just don't want to step on a grape with a
Bare foot — so I scanned the carpet and the
Wood floor without success — and turned about

In frustration putting my life on hold
Searching searching for the purple nuisance.

I slipped into
denial saying
there is
no
purple
grape.

I don't have to worry about why the
Cosmos has peopled the earth with humans
Because I am here as one among the
Billions of us — and I don't have to think

About my eyes and ears and tongue to make
Them work as they see and hear and taste with
No effort on my part — there is sight and
Sound and taste and consciousness coming with

Life — and even with my dreaming at night
I cannot separate myself from the
Nature of my being — I breath and the
Sun burns and I can imagine the crest

Of sunlight perpetually breaking
Over the earth — turning the night to day.

I don't have to
worry so much
because I'm coming
to believe consciousness
is indestructible.

Johnnie the cat in his elder years has
Developed a habit of yowling for
His food as he anticipates being
Forgotten and it is damn annoying

To hear him — and he won't stop when I say
NO — and it's better to ignore the noise
While feeding him but yesterday I sang
Daba daba daba daba — eeyoow —

Daba daba daba daba — eeyoow —
Daba daba daba daba — eeeyooow —
Daba daba daba daba daba
Eeeyooow eeeyooow — so together we had

A little harmony and a test of
Dominance and Johnnie was the winner.

I'm cranky
but he thinks
he's starving.

How does my head look to my eyes — and may
I turn my head to see it better — or
Is it always beyond my seeing — or
Perhaps when I'm seeing pink rose petals

Dry on the concrete and the daylilies
Beginning to bloom — and see my mother
Becoming frailer with age in the home
Holding so many of our memories

And possessions — perhaps I am seeing
What there is to see — that everything lives
To blossom and pass away — and perhaps
It's better to relax and flow with the

Current — as I am a story I tell
Myself on the way to another birth?

But perhaps my
head contains the
cosmos that keeps
creating visions?

There are different rhythms to life and some
Are profound and seemingly eternal
Like the tide coming in and going out
In response to the movements of the moon

And the passing of a person into
The elements is a seemingly cruel
Transition because we don't remember
What the experience of dying is

Like — but the fear of the unknown can be
A source of stimulation because I
Learn this is a world where everything is
Changing into something else and maybe

I can find encouragement in the thought
Death is only a season of living.

The sight and song
of an indigo bunting
on the fly is a
glimpse of ephemeral
beauty.

Without the sensation of touching the
Sun would be neither warm nor cool and
Without the propensity of seeing
The sun would be neither bright nor dark as

I create the waves of light with my eyes
And I manifest the warmth of the sun
With my skin — and I appreciate the
Music of Beethoven with my ears — and

A peach would not be peachy without my
Tasting it — because it is my body
That makes seeing hearing touching tasting
Smelling and comprehending possible —

I am not even lifting a finger
And yet I'm bringing the cosmos to life.

I don't have to
worry about birth
as it keeps on
happening.

Henry is a white cat with orange spots
And he is missing the tips of his ears
Because they were frozen off while he was
Living outside in the winter — and a

Friend allowed him inside and took care of
Him — and I have had him for many years
And he developed kidney disease so
Every morning with my hand I scoop him

Up from bed and take him to the kitchen
Where from behind him I leverage his face back
And squirt some medicine down his throat with
A syringe — which he doesn't like so much —

But the sticky stuff keeps him from getting
Constipated and permits him to eat.

He makes
growly
raspy
curmudgeonly
commentary.

I have been driving around and seeing
The scenery of city streets and of
The highway and listening to disks of
Alan Watts who was a beatnik guru

Telling me that within my head there is
Hidden a hintergedanken — meaning
That there is something that I know but will
Not admit — and it's not a trivial

Thing like knowing I need to lose weight or
To pay for the registration of my
Car again — and it's not admitting that
I'm a drunk because I've already done

That — this hintergedanken is so much
More fundamentally liberating.

Alan is exposing
the riddling tricks
of gurus so maybe
he's playing a
trick on me.

There is the nagging intuition that
Life is more than the satisfactions of
Eating and having sex but I can't put
My finger on what's the bigger deal and

Alan says that I am continuous
And interdependent with everything
Else — so much so that if you were not you
I would not be who I am — and Alan

Is saying that part of me knows the whole
Cosmos is seeing with my eyes but when
I am trying by an act of will to grasp
Enlightenment frustration arises —

The hintergedanken is Alan's way
Of suggesting wisdom before knowledge.

Driving around and
listening to Alan
inspires
unexplainable
joy.

When we drunks talk among ourselves with the
Intention of perpetuating our
Sobriety sometimes one of us will
Confidently repeat a point — as if

By the elaboration and by the
Assertion of his words he could transform —
And from my experience I know that
I need to listen carefully to the

Words that come out of me — and it is true
Sometimes I can talk myself into a
Better way of feeling as my words give
Me the leverage I need to strengthen

My intentions to remember that a
World of misery comes with the first drink.

Some of us
are treading
water over a bottomless
pit and the words we
choose are pivotal.

An onion is a handy symbol for
Life because there are the layers of skin
That can be peeled away until at the
Center nothing remains — so the thing to

Do is to cut the skins and mix them with
Other ingredients and savor their
Taste and digest the onion — there is the
Illusion that I can peel away the

Surfaces of things to find a hidden
Truth after which there is satisfaction —
Can I savor the skin after skin
And be satisfied with the taste of life

Without grasping for explanations — as
If my tasting weren't miracle enough?

With telescopes and
microscopes we chase
the cosmos and it
keeps on
evading.

There was a time my Dad told me that he
Didn't believe in an afterlife and
That when we die we go to a void — and
His saying so was a revelation

To me — that he was a Christian who was
Ministering to a congregation
From a pulpit while not believing in
The resurrection — that he viewed himself

As a Roman stoic who thought that the
Consolations of the gospels were a
Crutch for a weaker sort of people — and
I understand the vehemence of his

Need to be important and the stress he
Placed upon having righteous opinions.

Today I believe
he frightened
himself to
death.

There is so much sunlight in July from
The early hours of the morning on
Into the shadowing of the evening
That the grass and the trees and the sky are

Transformed into a glowing presence and
Today there is an occasional breeze
In the leaves and the air is suffused with
A dry heat that is a pleasure to feel

And everything that I see is tinged in
A yellow light and the air is alive
With flying insects from the smallest gnats
To the speeding flies vanishing and three

Crows are flying in circles and chasing
Each other twice among the quiet leaves.

After forty minutes
of meditation all
my sensations are
drinking in a
summer morning.

I don't know what a Roman stoic
Was and I don't believe my Dad really
Did either because he could only have
Read about them in books after they died

Thousands of years ago and the earth has
Moved on and so my Dad was expressing
A rejection of his perception of
His intellectual surroundings — which

Is sad — because an unresolved fear of
Oblivion drove his thinking — like a
Person who is slowly drowning — while I'm
Trying to awake and discover that

The void is pregnant with consciousness and
Birth is a gift that keeps on happening.

My dad was terrified of
graves but with practice I don't
need explanations and
rationalizations as
persisting joy arises.

I return to the question does the world
Exist apart from me or do we both
Arise together inseparable —
While the patterns of my living with my

Perceptions and reactions and all the
Elements of my identity are
Destined to dissolve as transitory
As a season's leafing — along with a

Listing of accomplishments that only
I am capable of remembering with
Dubious accuracy — all the while
There is an irrepressible birthing

Going on coming from a void bestowing
Such rejuvenating forgetfulness?

Am I really by
myself beating my
heart or is the
whole cosmos
beating my heart?

The sun is baking my head while I am
At my desk and it's taking an effort
Of will to focus my thoughts while it is
So much easier to notice the heat

About my face and neck and under my
Arms as I am beginning to sweat in
The moisture of this morning's heat — while the
The plants outside the window are growing

Riotously after a night of rain
And thunder with the radiation and
Radiation bearing down on the land
And fetching the biting mosquitoes and

Flies and irritation is easy and
So I'm just going to be irritated.

At my desk I raise
my feet and lower
my toes — my clogs
fall off and my feet are
bare joyously.

Six months ago the temperature was
Twenty below zero but today I
Am wearing clogs — which are a glorious
Invention — because they allow all the

Benefits of going barefoot without
Drawbacks — as I enjoy lifting my heels
While sitting down and feeling the heat of
The summer air envelope my ankles

And by lowering my toes the clogs will
Drop and my feet obtain liberation —
I don't have to poke my skin by walking
Over rocks — and don't have to smear my feet

With dirt — and if a pebble gets under
A foot I tilt and the pebble falls out.

The clogs that were
left behind at a hotel
and given to me are
two sizes too big — so
I am duckish.

When I am thinking about myself and
All the unfortunate things that happened
To me and about how a certain girl
Treated me it is natural to fall

Into a gruesome mood as if I were
A whirlpool swirling uselessly and
Wasting the marvelous unfolding of
The cosmos as it appears at the moment

So it's much better to see the cobwebs
In the corner of a window wafting
In a breeze that the air conditioner
Is raising or to enjoy the design

Of my clogs that I may wear or dispense
With — indulging my fickle summer moods.

There is so much
possession and
defending going
on in thinking
about myself.

I put my chin in the cup of my palm
While looking out of the window — and I
Am thinking of nothing especially
Important — and the sun is declining

Behind me as the green of the leaves and
The white of the clouds and the blue of the
Sky are untouched by the evening shadows —
There are the hums in the room emitted

By the refrigerator the printer
And the aquarium — particles are
Cresting from the sky and bouncing off of
The clouds and leaves and I am creating

A spectrum of light — and vibrations are
Undulating and I am making sound.

Rippling thoughts are
leaving traces
in the form of
some words on
paper.

The gray of the clouds is pregnant with rain
And the rain may burst at any moment
And I'm waiting for something to happen
Anticipating a sudden downpour

And the tiny white blooms of the clover
Are ascending above the blades of grass
And there is just enough breeze stirring the
Leaves to make the quiet more prominent —

There's not a bird in sight — not a squirrel
Anywhere — a hundred thousand blades of
Grass — a hundred thousand leaves — are waiting —
Gloom is descending — chill is engulfing —

Butterflies and dragonflies are grounded
And not a drop of rain has fallen yet.

Dark patches of the
overcast sky are
moving swiftly.

Bayport Minnesota and Hutchison
Kansas are alive in me — not as they
Are today but how they were forty and
Fifty years ago — and I remember

My first friend Eric — though probably I
Wouldn't recognize him today — and there
Are many painful memories as it's
Easy to recall my disappointments —

And as I keep going on and on there
Is more and more to remember though I
Suspect I've forgotten most of my life —
And I wonder whether I am choosing

What to recall and what to forget or
Is memory something that just happens?

I am happy to be
a soap bubble person
ready to disappear
to be born again
for another game.

There are islands of shade under the pines
The apple trees and the cottonwood but
The remainder of the lawn is exposed
To the blaze of the sun as the gripping

Treads of the front two self-propelled wheels of
My mower are pulling me along and
Covering the grass with two whirling blades
As I am enveloped and baking in

The moist air of a July afternoon
Happy that I had sawed off the lower
Limbs of the apple trees and the pines so
That I could move rapidly without a

Hindrance and to impose my will and to
Establish order on my property.

Kentucky blue grass
creeping Charlie
dandelions
and clover are
all the same to me.

The blazing sun
is concealed by
threatening clouds
as heat continues
into evening.

— *Tekkan*

www.ingramcontent.com/pod-product-compliance
Lightning Source LLC
Chambersburg PA
CBHW042117100526
44587CB00025B/4099